Eternity Calls

Grace Barnes
She lived her dream

As told by

Norman Barnes

Eternity Calls

Copyright © 2023 Norman Barnes

First Edition

First published 2023

The moral rights of the author have been asserted.

This work is protected by copyright law.

All rights reserved.

CC BY-NC-ND 4.0.

All content enquiries to norman@destinycalls.org

Scripture quotations are taken from The Holy Bible,

New International Version® NIV®

Copyright © 1973 1978 1984 2011

Biblica, Inc.

Used with permission.

All rights reserved worldwide.

ISBN: 9798376126035

Dedication

If Grace were here, she would dedicate this book to Christian women who are hesitant about stepping out in their ministries.

Remember the saying, 'If Grace can do it, so can I.'

Acknowledgements

I would like to thank the hundreds of family members and friends who have supported me in many different ways since Grace departed.

And especially to Becca Jupp, leader of Arun Church for her kindness and unwavering faith; to Cleland Thom for co-writing this book; and to Jenn Harborth, of Clean Copy Proofreading, for editing and publishing it.

I am deeply grateful to you all.

Donations

Links International has set up a special fund in Grace's memory.

Donations should go to:

Links International – Projects account

Account number: 00432695

Sort code: 30-99-86

Ref: Grace Memorial Fund

Contents

Dedication i

Acknowledgements ii

Contents iii

Chapter 1 The Day Eternity Called 1

Chapter 2 How It All Began 4

Chapter 3 Love and Marriage 9

Chapter 4 God's Work 16

Chapter 5 More Than One Way to Have Children 20

Chapter 6 A Lady of Many Talents 33

Chapter 7 Pioneering Overseas 41

Chapter 8 Pioneering With Women 46

Chapter 9 Forming Links 50

Chapter 10 How Ordinary Are You? 53

Chapter 11 The American Dream 59

Chapter 12 Later Years 69

Chapter 13 The End…and the Beginning 75

Tributes to Grace 83

Chapter 1

The Day Eternity Called

Going to meet Jesus

Friday, 9 September 2022, was just another day. And then the phone rang. It was the call that I had dreaded – summoning me urgently to Worthing Hospital, where Grace was seriously ill.

When I arrived, the consultant told me that she was going to die. She had sustained a massive heart attack due to shock after falling and breaking her femur in our flat a week earlier.

Choking back the tears, I went into the intensive care unit. Grace was sitting up in bed. She looked at me and said, 'I am going to die, Norman. But I'm not afraid – I am at perfect peace. I am going to heaven, and I will meet Jesus.'

We chatted for a while, and she prayed and thanked the Lord for our 58 years of marriage and the way I had cared for her.

Then I prayed for her and gave her to the Lord whom we both loved so much. I asked her if she wanted me to sit with her and hold her hand.

But she said, 'No, let's kiss goodbye and you can go home. Then I will go to be with the Lord.'

As I left the room, I looked back and she blew me a kiss and waved. That was the last time I saw her.

Three hours later, she went to be with her God. Eternity had called.

Grace finished strong, she ran the race and was ready to meet him.

What a loss

That day, I lost my best friend, my soulmate, my wife and much more. It's impossible to describe what this diminutive lady meant to me.

And, the Links family lost one of its founders and its matriarch. Hundreds, even thousands of people across the world lost their spiritual mother and grandmother, their prayer champion, their friend, and their greatest and most devoted advocate.

Hebrews 13:7 says, 'Remember your leaders, who spoke the word of God to you. Consider the outcome of their way of life and imitate their faith.'

Grace's life is certainly worth remembering, not just as words in this book, but as treasure in our hearts. Her impact will resonate around the world for years to come.

It was a life worth imitating. A life that was a consistent and faithful testimony to the power and grace of God.

She was a survivor, too – a trooper and a great leader who learned to press through difficult circumstances and who overcame so many difficulties, such as dyslexia and major surgery.

Grace survived the Second World War as a young girl in London and later followed God's call to minister in some dangerous nations.

She had a courageous faith that challenged everyone who knew her to aspire to greater things. She overcame hardships and trials, and she never stopped pointing people to Jesus. For her, he was the one who made it all possible, the only reason for living.

We often joked about our funerals, and she said that I would need to book the Royal Albert Hall for mine.

It never occurred to her that she might need a large venue too. She was truly humble and self-effacing and never realised how many people she had influenced.

I fondly called her Dolly, and during our 58 years together, we experienced times of great joy and sadness, pain and delight. We travelled the world and stayed in some of the best hotels as well as primitive mud huts.

We prayed every day that we would finish strong: physically, mentally, emotionally and spiritually. And Grace did just that.

Chapter 2

How It All Began

Grace's early years

God had his hand on Grace, from the moment she was born. He even chose her name.

Her mum and dad had planned to call her Audrey, but she nearly died at birth. The doctor told her parents, 'It's only by God's grace you've got this child.' So, they called her Grace, a name that turned out to be deeply appropriate.

Like many of God's giants, she came from very humble beginnings. She was a true Cockney, born in Whitechapel, east London. Her father was a porter in Borough Market, and her mother was a devout Anglican. But God put Grace on his apprenticeship programme when she was very young.

You won't find that programme in any training manual and, if you do, it won't have many recruits. It's called servanthood. And the syllabus involves sacrificial giving, unconditional caring and loving the unloved.

That's what Grace did for the whole of her life.

Her family moved to Dagenham when she was two, and, as a child and teenager, she helped her mother care for her elderly grandparents. She ran errands, helped with the housework, and looked after them when they were ill.

During the war, she went with her mum and dad to the Air Raid Precautions station where babies and young children were taken after their homes were bombed. She helped to feed the children and played with them, often just minutes after their parents had been killed… a tough task at a tough time.

When Grace was 17, she looked after her elderly grandmother who was too ill to care for herself. Grace nursed her until she died. Those early lessons prepared her for the works of love that continued, almost to the day she died.

The woman I fell in love with – Grace aged 25 at her home in Dagenham, Essex

Uneducated – but intelligent

Grace had very little education as her schooling had been virtually wiped out by the war. But there's a difference between education and intelligence, and what Grace lacked in one, she more than made up for in the other. She had profound wisdom and often out-thought the finest minds.

When we went to Chadwell Christian Mission in 1966, I was the 'pastor', but Grace did much of the pastoral work. She inherited a ladies' group that mainly comprised elderly women, and she faithfully did their washing every Monday. Our kitchen looked like a Chinese laundry.

And she cooked meals for all and sundry. People frequently popped in for a bite to eat.

And wherever we lived, we tried to stay true to those east London roots. Our front door and our fridge door were always open to callers, and we loved people dropping in.

Grace used to say, 'We want people to be relaxed and comfortable. We don't ask anyone to take their shoes off or anything like that. Our home is God's. We welcome people as they are, the same as he does.'

I will never be able to replace her ministry as a 'hostess' and don't intend to try – I can guarantee that my cooking isn't in the same league as hers, though I have tried to follow her legendary recipe for shepherd's pie!

But I'll be keeping the front door open, even if I ask people to pick up a takeaway before they arrive.

At our house in Chadwell Heath, Essex

God's call

God gave Grace a vision for her life before he started work on me.

She was saved when she was 11 and baptised in the Spirit a couple of years later. She went to Bethel Pentecostal Church in Dagenham and made several good friends at the youth prayer meetings and Bible study.

One week a friend named Kathy Lucas had a vision to go to Africa. Grace was thrilled for her but felt sad, too, as she couldn't see God using her like that. She didn't have a very high opinion of herself. In contrast, Kathy had been to a grammar school and had good reading and writing skills.

Soon afterwards, Grace went for a walk in Pondfield Park, Dagenham and cried out to God, 'What have you got for me? How will you use me?'

God's answer came quickly and clearly as Grace walked along the path between the trees. He said, 'You will travel the world and live out of a suitcase.'

Years later, in 1990, Grace and I went to the Congo, and Grace spoke at a women's meeting. Afterwards, someone came up to her and said, 'You remind me of another woman who spoke here.' This woman turned out to be – Kathy Lucas!

Grace was dumbstruck. Kathy had made it to Africa, too, and served God there for 35 years before retiring. And Grace got there too.

And you can imagine the smile on God's face as he whispered to Grace, 'I kept my promise.'

Chapter 3

Love and Marriage

Mum's the word

Mothers have high hopes for their sons, and my mum was no exception.

She also had a habit of knowing more about my future than I did, and she picked Grace out as my future wife long before I even thought about it.

Grace started going to Bethel Pentecostal church in Dagenham when she was 24. But the nearby Elim Pentecostal Church in Dagenham urgently needed Sunday school teachers, so she decided to help, and she told Bethel's minister she was leaving. He wasn't too pleased, but her mind was made up and off she went.

My mum, who went to this church too, spotted Grace on her first day there. She quickly decided that Grace was the right girl for her Norman. How did she know? She had not even spoken to the girl. But God had evidently spoken to her, and she prayed enthusiastically about a possible relationship. I'm glad she did!

First impressions

I got to know Grace when she came to the church's 7am prayer meetings that I arranged on Sundays. I thought to myself, 'Anyone that comes to a prayer meeting at this time of day is my kind of girl.'

When she first met me, she thought I was the most big-headed person she had ever encountered. Her view was that this Norman Barnes knew everything, always wanted to take charge and was more than secure in who he was. I freely admit she was right.

I also had this habit of kissing the girls hello and goodbye. A holy kiss, of course! But Grace made it plain through friends that, if I tried it with her, I would get a smack around the face. I got the message, and I didn't dare find out if she meant it.

But a romance blossomed, and within six months we got engaged. But I was only 18 and, since Grace was a very proper lady, she decided we could not marry until I was 21.

That was in 1964, the year the Beatles were starting out on their road to fame. My mum's first impression had been fulfilled.

Grace on our wedding day in 1964

Bread from heaven

We had a wonderful wedding day at the Elim Pentecostal Church in Dagenham. It was one of those occasions when you sensed a twinkle in God's eye.

But reality soon struck – we had to end our honeymoon early when we ran out of money. We had a halfpenny between us. And when we arrived back at our rented flat, we didn't have any food, either. So, we prayed and decided to go and see my mum.

We didn't tell her about our predicament, but she unexpectedly gave us a load of groceries she had received in an offer at the supermarket. We accepted them gratefully, and that was how we began our walk of faith.

We often had to 'pray in' our food, and our faith grew as we learned to trust God in small things. It was exciting, though scary at times.

Twice, we sat down to eat dinner off empty plates, as we didn't have any food to put on them.

The first time, we had our tithe money in a tin, but we were determined not to spend it. So, we prayed, and our landlord knocked on the door.

'Do you fancy a couple of plates of stew?' he asked. 'My wife has cooked too much, and we've got some to spare.' Needless to say, we said yes. It was lovely.

The second time, we could only find vegetables for dinner, and I wasn't ready to become a vegetarian. But then an old school friend, Brian Davis, stopped by. 'God told me to buy you some steak,' he announced, and he plonked a bag containing two lovely steaks on the table. You never forget things like that. Our faith was growing, and God was preparing us for the future.

Once, we needed to go to a meeting, which was three miles away, but the tank on our motorbike was bone dry and we didn't have any money for petrol.

I was indoors wondering what to do, when I glanced out of the window and saw Grace in the street, laying hands on the motorbike and praying over it. I couldn't recall anything quite like that in scripture (apart from the 'roar of Moses' Triumph!') – but I had a choice. I could either go out, put my arm around her and say, 'Nice try, love.' Or I could stand with her in faith.

I chose the faith option. We put on our motorcycle gear, got on the bike, kicked the pedal, and it started. And it kept going, without any fuel, for another three days.

Eventually, some money arrived in the post, so I drove to the garage, and the 'prayer-fuel' ran out just as I pulled up at the pump. As the price of petrol increased, I sometimes wished Grace would pray like that more often!

Later, we drew on those lessons in impossible situations both at home and across the world.

And it was so rewarding to share our stories with younger Christians and impart faith to them. Grace continued doing this in one way or another, right to the day she died.

Younger generations may need to recall those faith stories in the tough economic times that lie ahead.

And as they step out like we did, they will meet the same God who meets all their needs according to his riches in Christ Jesus.

Our dream home?

Most married couples dream of owning a house. We were no different and made tentative enquiries about buying somewhere. But I didn't earn enough for a mortgage, so we reluctantly dropped the idea.

However, we heard there was a flat available to rent a few miles away, but we discovered that 100 people had applied for it. We joined them and made it to the shortlist – just us and another couple.

We fully believed that God had given us the flat but, just to be on the safe side, we prayed, 'Lord, if it's not your will, we don't want it.'

We didn't really mean it, though. So, when we heard that the flat had gone to the other couple, we hit rock bottom.

My mum was disappointed, too. My sister had bought her own house and Mum felt it wasn't fair.

In desperation, she prayed, 'Lord, Norman and Grace love and serve you but don't even have a home of their own. That can't be right.'

As she prayed, God gave her a vision of a building with a hall and a stage. The stage had blue curtains, and the hall had brown chairs. There was a two-bedroom flat attached to the building.

The vision was so vivid that she confidently told us, 'Norman, you're going to be a pastor.' I was angry and told her, in no uncertain terms, 'I don't want to be a pastor, I want to be an evangelist.' But she held the dream in her heart and prayed about it. And, as usual, she was right!

Grace in her younger days

Chapter 4

God's Work

The job I didn't want

Our good friend John Noble was invited to be pastor of the Chadwell Christian Mission, in Chadwell Heath, east London. He turned the offer down but said that Grace and I might be suitable.

The trustees invited me to preach, and my mum and dad came along, too. As we walked into the building, Mum said, 'This is the place I saw in the vision.' She asked the secretary if there was a two-bedroom flat attached to the building. There was.

'You will be pastor here one day,' she told me.

'I will not,' I replied, angrily. 'I've told you before, I don't want to be a pastor. I've got no time for it, and certainly not here. I don't want to care for all these old people. Anyway, they haven't invited me.'

'They will,' Mum replied, with infuriating confidence.

And, again, she was right. I received a letter inviting me to be their pastor. It was ridiculous. I was only 24 and a dedicated Pentecostal. But with Grace's encouragement, I accepted the offer.

And so, we had a flat of our own. As usual, God did it his way.

Grace with our dog Tim in the garden of our church, Oasis House, in Chadwell Heath

Grace finds grace

Grace loved the flat, but she was petrified about being a pastor's wife. She knew she had to look and act the part, even though she didn't feel comfortable with it. So, she studied other ministers' wives, noting how they managed to smile in public, and how they never raised their voices and never lost their cool.

Grace didn't find this easy, as she was down-to-earth and said what she felt. But she eventually succeeded in presenting the right image most of the time.

Once, she was invited to a women's World Day of Prayer. It was bitterly cold with snow on the ground, so she put on boots, a scarf and a winter coat. But all the other women arrived wearing their finest apparel, leaving Grace feeling ashamed of her appearance.

While she was there, someone asked her where she was from, and when she told them, the lady replied, 'Oh, they have a new minister.'

'Yes, that's right,' Grace said, not giving anything away.

'Could you ask the minister's wife if she would come and speak to this group?' the lady asked.

'Of course,' Grace promised.

The minister's wife duly accepted the invitation and Grace returned to speak, dressed in all *her* finery.

Hard times

Most of the folk at the mission were elderly, and Grace and I learned to care for them. I was reluctant, but it came naturally to Grace.

We often sat through the night as people lay dying, and then we laid them out for their funerals.

In fact, we were so good at it, the local undertaker offered us some work.

It was traumatic, but we learned a lot about God, the reality of the gospel and of knowing his peace in people's final hours. Grace was well prepared when her turn came to go to glory.

Caring for people took its toll, though. A member of the mission became ill, and we sat up all night, caring and praying for him. Then, in the morning, I went to work. This went on for three days and nights. I didn't sleep at all.

One day, while I was working on a roof, I found myself struggling to stay awake. It dawned on me that I might be overdoing it. Fortunately, though, I did not fall off! That would have given a whole new meaning to the expression 'dropping off to sleep'.

But when I arrived home, Grace opened the front door, and I pitched forward and fell headlong into the hallway. She managed to drag me to bed where I slept for 24 hours. She momentarily wondered if I was dead.

I eventually woke up, had something to eat and then slept for another 24 hours. I am convinced that long sleep saved me from a breakdown.

I am still grateful for the way Grace looked after me during that time. It came naturally to her. She was a true servant.

Chapter 5

A Different Kind of Family

Coping with loss

We were delighted when Grace conceived our first baby. But then, sadly, she lost it.

Grace had a history of fibroids. She needed an operation when she was two and another when she was 24. But the problem returned and caused the miscarriage. Knowing the reason did not make the loss any easier.

A specialist from the Royal London Hospital came to our flat to examine her and told us, 'It's very unlikely that you will ever have children.'

Those stark words hit us like shock waves from an exploding bomb. We were dazed. Stunned. Numb.

After the consultant left, we fell into each other's arms and wept. We tried to console one another over the next few days, but it was an empty, hopeless time.

We clung to the faint hope of a miracle, but our dream of having children lay shattered. We cried from our hearts, 'Why us?' We couldn't understand what childlessness would achieve. Why was God asking this of us?

Our disappointment turned to anger. 'What kind of God are you?' we cried in frustration. 'We've given up everything for your sake and now you are asking this of us.'

Grace battles on

In 1978, any lingering hopes of having children disappeared when Grace was taken to hospital for a hysterectomy.

But there were complications. Her bowel had collapsed because she had already had so many operations, and her condition became critical. A surgeon was rushed through London with a police escort to carry out emergency surgery.

Grace was at death's door. At home, folk prayed, while two surgeons operated on her, one working on the collapsed bowel and the other performing the hysterectomy. It was a miracle she survived.

But Grace was a fighter. She resolved to be up and walking around the ward by the next day. And by noon she had done it. She was equally determined not to let the operation demoralise her. So, she went around the other wards speaking to the patients and praying with them.

Compassion in action

A teenaged girl in the bed opposite was boasting that she had had two abortions, and her words had pierced Grace's heart like a knife.

Grace's initial reaction was not very 'Christian'! It had seemed so unfair that this girl had aborted two babies when Grace could not have even one.

But Grace realised this young girl needed love. She couldn't allow bitterness to take root in her heart. So, she went across to the girl's bed and put her arms around her. The girl wept. Her boasting had been just a cover for her true feelings.

Even in those darkest moments, God's light dispelled some black and ominous clouds.

God had other plans

At her lowest point, Grace recalled God asking her many years earlier, 'Are you prepared to give up everything for me?'

Grace had pondered before answering, 'Yes Lord, apart from having a family. You wouldn't expect me to do that, would you? After all, that's what you created us for, isn't it?'

But God had other plans. We never knew why, and it cost us a great deal.

Eventually, we found peace. We said 'Yes' to God's will, but we added the proviso, 'Lord, if you are really asking this of us, we ask for your grace to accept it. And we also ask for a spiritual family – sons and daughters in the kingdom of God.'

God heard that prayer and answered it in many ways. But Grace carried the pain of being unable to have children for the rest of her life.

New kinds of parents

God used the young people at the mission to answer our cry for spiritual sons and daughters. But this was not the only way he answered our prayers.

The turning point came when our good friends John and Chris Norton had a baby girl called Victoria, Vicky for short. They involved us in almost every aspect of her life.

And after Vicky was weaned, John and Chris put a cot in our home so she could spend nights with us. We also took her to the nursery and bought things for her. Their selflessness filled huge gaps in our lives.

But it wasn't easy. We had to make ourselves vulnerable and expose the tender areas of our hearts, places that many people without children avoid because it's too painful.

Pushing someone else's child down the road in a pram could have been upsetting. But we learned to face our insecurity and pain, find God in our weakness, and receive his healing and his grace. And he was faithful.

Vicky is now married to James, and they have three children of their own. We felt so privileged that we were able to sow some seeds in her life. She still remembers coming to our flat for those 'special weekends'. They were special for us, too.

Vicky wasn't the only baby we cared for. Grace looked after another child for a while because the mother couldn't cope with it. To me, this really was church in action, and everyone benefited.

Adapt or adopt?

There was a 16-year-old girl named Sue at the mission and I called her into my vestry one day. She had looked sad in the meeting, and I wanted to see if there was anything wrong.

She explained that her mother and stepfather were emigrating to Australia, and she didn't want to go. She was courting a young man called Terry and did not want to lose him. And she wanted to keep her job.

I told her that if she ended up with nowhere to stay, Grace and I would be happy for her to live with us. It was one of those emotional moments when you say things you later regret. And regret it, I did.

It wasn't long before her angry mother was banging on our front door. 'What do you think you are doing?' she exploded as she marched into the house.

'What do you mean?' I asked, bewildered by this full-on attack.

'Sue says she doesn't have to go to Australia, because you will look after her. What on earth gives you the right to interfere in our family life? I am trying to keep the family together, and here you are, doing exactly the opposite.'

I had to eat humble pie and apologise. I lacked Grace's wisdom on that occasion.

At about the same time, my brother-in-law, who worked for social services, asked us to foster a young girl. We were reluctant. We had tried to adopt children but had been turned down because of our low income and because we didn't own our own home.

We had considered fostering but felt unable to cope with the emotional turmoil of caring for a child and then having to say goodbye. But this was to be long-term fostering. So, we agreed.

The day before we were due to sign the fostering papers, a lady in our church phoned Grace. At the end of the conversation, she made a chance remark, 'I hear you are going to have a young girl living with you.'

'Oh, yes,' said Grace, thinking about the girl we were about to foster. But the lady continued, 'Sue's mum told me that she is coming to live with you.'

Grace couldn't believe her ears. Now it was my turn to bang on Sue's front door to ask her mother what was going on.

'Oh yes,' she said. 'We thought it was a good idea and decided to take you up on your offer.'

So, we cancelled the plan to foster the other girl, and Sue moved in with us.

Our family begins

The first year was hard, and we all had to adapt.

We suddenly had a teenaged girl thrust on us, with all the problems that can bring. And Sue had to get used to our hectic lifestyle, which was different from anything she had known.

We didn't pressure Sue to become a Christian. We just encouraged her to be part of our lives and she began to trust us as she got to know us.

Grace was amazing with her. She was a natural mum, with endless love and patience as well as firm words when necessary!

Then, the year after Sue moved in, something remarkable happened among the 12 young people in our church's Bible class. One Sunday, God gave me a prophetic word for each person.

The next day, Sue came home and was very quiet. We realised that God was speaking to her. The following evening, she came to us and said, 'I've sorted it out. I want to become a Christian. Terry doesn't want to become a Christian, but I'm leaving that with him. I want to go on with God.'

Within a day or two, Terry contacted us and told us that he wanted to become a Christian, too. So, we had the joy of leading them both to the Lord. Our spiritual family had started.

The following Sunday, Sue and Terry gave their testimonies, and, over the next month, 10 other young people were saved, baptised, and filled with the Holy Spirit. We suddenly had more 'sons and daughters' than we knew what to do with!

Sue lived with us for three years and became like a daughter to us. We helped to pay for her wedding.

The newly-weds moved into a house in Kinfauns Road, and later on, we bought a house almost opposite. Several other church members also lived nearby. A real community was growing.

Next, we were grandparents

Before long, Sue became pregnant with Stephanie, and someone in the church asked her where Grace and I would fit into the picture when Stephanie was born.

Sue replied, in all naivety, 'Oh, they can choose what they want to be called, nana and grandpa, or grandma and granddad.'

She had already counted us in. So, we became grandma and granddad to little Stephanie. And our connection with Sue and Terry didn't end there.

Sue had trouble falling pregnant with her second child, so we all prayed and fasted one day a week for five years. And eventually, God answered, and Stephanie's brother Paul was born.

What's in a name?

Even though we had been turned down for adoption, God had other ideas.

We had started helping a church in Kwadaso, Ghana, and made close friends there, including Johnny Baduh and his wife who had a little girl.

Now, in Ghana, they traditionally name their children after people whom they wish to honour, and the couple were expected to name the girl after her grandmother.

But Johnny flatly refused. The grandmother was dead, and he did not want his daughter named after a dead person. He wanted to name her after somebody he honoured and who was alive.

'I want to call my little daughter after Mama Barnes,' he declared. He wanted to honour the way that Grace, a white woman, had gone to Ghana and shown them love, care and concern.

It was moving for Grace, especially when she heard that the little girl had been named 'Grace Barnes' at her dedication.

And as she grew up, the girl was often asked, 'What is your African name?' And she would proudly tell them, 'Grace Barnes.'

So, God heard our cry and gave us children.

Grace mark 2 now has a management degree and is married to a pastor in the Church of Pentecost,. They have a son.

We were so proud of them and could not have loved them more if they had been our own children.

So, we ended up with nephews and nieces, children and grandchildren. This included two other little African children who were named after us; over the years we paid for their education. What a great way to invest money.

Our baby 'grandson' Oscar

Helping others have children

Grace and I often found that people were powerfully affected when we prayed for them to have children. Sometimes God gave us prophetic words for them, telling them to trust him for children. And he did the rest.

Remarkably, we were always able to rejoice with them when those prayers were answered, without feeling resentful or jealous. I guess that's because of the healing God brought to our lives. But sometimes we became very emotional.

We learned that God accepted that we needed to weep. But he encouraged us not to become bitter, because bitterness will destroy you and everyone around you.

It was a sin and must be confessed and repented.

God gave Grace a precious ministry in praying for childless women, even though – or maybe because – she couldn't have children herself.

In February 1997, we visited Bridge Church in Brentford, and Dr Patrick Dixon asked couples to come forward if they were unable to conceive. Twelve couples responded. Grace prayed for them, and we heard later that at least ten ladies became pregnant.

Another couple was initially unable to conceive, but eventually asked us to stop praying after they had their fourth child! Understandably, four was enough.

Grace also prayed for a childless couple at Grapevine in August 2007, and by April 2008, the lady had received a 'double portion' – she was pregnant with twins.

God's ways weren't ours

I have to say, though, that both Grace and I felt that all these miracles never compensated for the fact that we did not have our own children. I still cannot fully understand why God did not bless us with them.

But, with God, there are things we don't know and shouldn't know. Being childless freed us to travel, give more time to the Lord, look after children from broken homes and serve parents in the church.

But nothing ever filled the void in our hearts. We used to feel hurt when we heard parents talking about their children. And later we felt the same hurt when grandparents talked about their grandchildren.

If we could rerun history, we would choose to have children every time. But God gives you the grace to cope. This isn't a one-off 'zap', but something you draw on continually, minute by minute and day by day. It's not easy when you're hurting so deeply.

Why us?

People asked why God used me and Grace to help other childless couples. We believed we were stepping on the enemy's neck. If we couldn't have children, then we would help to extend God's kingdom by praying for others to have them instead.

And we continued to pray for these couples, as well as pregnant women, mothers, and their babies, right until Grace died.

Those prayers weren't always answered, and we sometimes helped couples who were struggling with the grim reality of childlessness.

We tried to pass on what we had learned when we walked through that black valley of despair. And we saw God fill that emptiness in people's hearts time and again.

But now, Grace is in heaven, the place where 'He will wipe every tear from their eyes. There will be no more death or mourning or crying or pain, for the old order of things has passed away' (Revelation 21:4).

It's a great relief to know she doesn't have to bear that pain any longer.

Chapter 6

A Lady of Many Talents

Expert host

Grace excelled at hospitality, and her gift affected people more than she realised. She treated everyone like royalty, whether they were nationally known figures or ex-convicts. She hosted both!

She gave every visitor the five-star treatment – a delicious, lovingly prepared three-course meal with wine, preceded by sherry and aperitifs, and followed by dessert, coffee, and sweets – all presented with a warmth and style that would impress the best hotels.

One man commented, 'I felt like I was the most important person on earth.' Another was reduced to tears when Grace produced a champagne breakfast on his 65th birthday.

Grace knew how to honour people, even if the freezer was almost empty. That's because she learned in some extraordinary circumstances.

She once visited a Bible school in Monterrey, Mexico, and she was deeply moved when the students gave up their own food so that she could eat.

It was a lesson that she never forgot. She discovered that if you give other people your last portion, then God will provide for you.

Later during the same trip, she was invited to a wealthy couple's house for lunch. As she entered their luxurious hallway, she noticed a dog basket on the floor. A little girl jumped out of the basket and offered her a drink.

The little girl was the couple's servant, and she slept in that basket. She had been one of Mexico's street children until the couple rescued her from a life of poverty, drugs, and sexual abuse.

Grace learned that day what a true servant heart looked like. She recalled, 'That experience showed me what it was to be free from slavery and to serve as a child of God.'

Creating, innovating

Grace was also a creative homemaker and could turn a room into a palace on a limited budget – and sometimes, with no budget at all.

Her creative streak came out in other ways, too, with her developing the creative arts in the church. When we first started at Chadwell Heath Mission, anything remotely artistic was labelled as 'worldly' or even 'of the devil'. So, Grace had a tough job getting people to overcome their fears and doctrinal hang-ups. But she persevered, and the mission soon became a place of innovation.

Her work grew, and we led creative weekends with other church groups. Some of the poetry, music and arts that you see in modern churches emerged from those meetings 40 years ago.

Many years later, when we were in America, Grace noticed that some churches were restricted in worship. Although they clapped and sang in the Spirit, they lacked other aspects, particularly creativity and the prophetic ministry.

We mentioned our concerns to the leaders to see how we could help, and they asked us to bring a team from back home to help them. So, Grace and I took musicians, dancers, a poet, and a worship leader over to Texas.

We left London with the temperature in the 60s and arrived at Dallas-Fort Worth to find it was 90°F plus. It was hot throughout our trip – the thermometer once touched 107°F. Thank God for cold drinks and air conditioning.

Grace was so excited about helping people to try out their creative gifts and was overjoyed when she saw them using them in her later visits.

Prayer and miracles

Miracles were part of Jesus' life and part of Grace's, too. We shared a longing to see God's healing power so that people would sit up and take notice.

And we were grateful for the isolated miracles we saw. We were moved when we saw suffering. Seeing someone in a wheelchair made us cry.

Once, at a women's conference in Brentwood, Essex, a woman asked for prayer. She had irons on both legs.

As Grace prayed, the woman's legs clicked back into place, and, when she got home, she took off the irons and walked normally. Later, she gave her testimony and danced, to prove what God had done.

Grace went to heaven praying and hoping to see more miracles and greater displays of God's power. That burden now falls on those of us who remain.

Prayer warrior

Grace certainly knew how to pray, and she was famous for her prayer board in the kitchen.

It was covered with photos of friends and family, young couples, teenagers, children, people who were not continuing with their faith, and children born to supposedly 'childless' women. There were even scans of unborn babies.

Most mornings, Grace got up and prayed passionately for them. And, while she shook the heavens with her prayers, I was usually shaking the pillow with my snores.

Then she would come in with a cup of tea and we would read the Bible and pray together.

We also read Psalm 91 out loud together every day. This Psalm was so important in Grace's life, and over the years she saw God keep every promise within it. So, it was fitting that our dear friend, John Thomas, read it with such love and conviction at her funeral.

I miss those morning routines and I have already made some changes. But I aim to keep praying for the people on Grace's prayer board with as much passion and diligence as she did.

A lady of love

Grace was and still is, loved all over the world. Thousands of men, women and children on almost every continent have been touched by her kindness and, sometimes, by her directness.

She saw life in black and white, with absolutely no shades of grey, but she said tough things kindly, which was a great gift.

I sometimes shuddered at the things she said to people, but she usually got away with it because people knew she wanted the best for them. She had no guile and simply said things how she saw them.

She was also my protector and got angry when people hurt me.

'I would like to wring their necks,' she would tell me when I had been badly treated or criticised.

But, fortunately for the people involved, she forgave them and took her anger and hurt to God.

She won't be able to protect me anymore, and I truly miss the one person who would defend me and watch out for me, even when I was wrong (although she would always put me straight later when we were alone!).

Grace and I worked together all over the world and in many different situations. Some leaders' wives are 'bolt-ons' to their husband's ministries. But Grace was different. We were bolted together.

Grace believed that God had called her to serve my ministry, and she was content to live in my shadow because I was more verbal and independent – a front man.

I remember her telling me, 'I don't mind that. Rather than restricting me, God has released me into a ministry of my own that I could never have imagined.'

God unites individuals' dreams and visions when people marry. It would have been difficult if I had travelled the globe while Grace stayed at home in front of the fire.

We fulfilled our callings in different ways because we were different people. But our gifts and characters complemented one another, and there was a supernatural synergy when we worked together. It's hard to be 'one flesh' if you're pulling in opposite directions.

We were often sad when we saw a husband tearing round the world doing 'God's work', while his angry and indifferent wife was stuck at home because she didn't share his vision, or he didn't want to take her with him. God never wanted it like that.

Reviving promises

Sometimes, during meetings we invited husbands and wives to face each other and lay hands on each other.

Then Grace would ask the wife to prophesy to her husband about the things that she longed to see happen in his life. Wives didn't find this too difficult.

Then we asked the husbands to do the same for their wives. Sadly, many were unaware of their wives' dreams or were selfishly pursuing their own goals while expecting their wives to trail along behind.

However, God often revived promises he had given couples when they were first converted, or when they got married, and Grace and I loved seeing this happen. In some cases, it's still happening – another part of her ongoing legacy.

The scripture says, 'Take delight in the Lord and he will give you the desires of your heart. Commit your way to the Lord; trust in him and he will do this' (Psalm 37:4-5).

Grace was living proof that these verses are true. And they will be true for anyone if they commit their way to the Lord, as she did.

Chapter 7

Pioneering Overseas

Affecting lives

Grace was quite literally a world-changer.

People often said, 'If Grace can do it, so can I.' And she took that as a huge compliment. She agreed that she was the last person you might expect God to use, especially in leadership roles or on public platforms.

But he used her anyway.

From a worldly perspective, 'successful' people are educated, come from the right background, and have proper 'training'.

But God often uses 'unqualified' people like Grace to make a powerful imprint on history.

She was dyslexic and found it hard to write and spell, but that didn't stop her from travelling to 47 countries. She spoke to a crowd of 70,000 at a women's conference in Ghana and chuckled because my biggest crowd was 'only' 14,000.

The country's first lady, Nana Konadu Agyeman-Rawlings had attended by helicopter. I couldn't match that, either!

Grace also led women's teams to Mexico, India, Burundi, Ghana, Sri Lanka, and Jamaica, and she encouraged those who felt they didn't have anything to contribute or were too afraid to step out.

She recalled, 'I made a point of recruiting women for my overseas teams who didn't usually do things or have any kind of public or leadership role.

'I loved encouraging them and giving them confidence. I told them that everyone has something to offer.

'My first job was to win their hearts, so they trusted me. And then I asked them to tell congregations a bit about themselves. By the end of the trip, some of them were giving testimonies, praying for people, or prophesying to them.

'But I never pushed them. Our job is to encourage people, not to push them.'

Grace earned women's friendship and respect by caring for them, and that needed some radical love at times.

Leading by example

While she was in Ghana, Grace asked co-worker Jane Lindsell if she would like her to wash her knickers.

Jane's response said it all. She said, 'If the team leader was prepared to wash my knickers, then I was more than happy to follow her.'

Grace also instructed her team to eat whatever was put in front of them while they were overseas.

But one woman found this a challenge too many when she accompanied Grace and her team into the African jungle.

Some village elders wanted to meet this white lady who was doing so much to help their people, and they served the customary African meal of rice and meat.

But they presented it in the customary way too – with cats and other animals jumping across the table.

The lady turned green when a mangy cat started eating the food off her plate. So, Grace quietly swapped plates and ate the cat's leftovers herself. That's what I call sacrifice.

Grace once told me, 'Some women were distressed because they didn't have a role in church. But I said that maybe God never intended that. Church leaders should remember that some women are called to influence the world, not the church.'

Grace was also an easy lady to underestimate, as any of the women who went on those teams will testify. She was very strict and disciplined, which is essential if you're going to survive in hostile climates and cultures.

Two were better than one

Grace travelled with me right from the start of my international work. We scarcely discussed whether she should come. Why wouldn't she?

She was always 100% behind everything I did but was equally happy to release me when I had to go away without her. Looking back, I suspect that, sometimes, she couldn't get me through the door fast enough!

She was content to stay at home to get on with things she didn't normally have time for. Sometimes she became a little impatient with wives who didn't like their husbands travelling as part of their work for God.

In her typical, forthright way, she told me, 'I can never understand them. Many men travel in the course of their jobs. Why should Christian men be any different? Travel is part and parcel of a leader's job, so wives should accept it. They are selfish.

'Some wives complain when their husband is away and, when he's at home, they expect him to pick the kids up from school. But churches don't pay their leaders to do that.

'I'm not like a widow who will never see her husband again. I find it easy to release you because I know you are coming back.'

And I have to say, she was wonderful to come back to, and I miss her cheery, 'Is that you, Norman?' when I arrive home.

I don't hear her say that anymore because *she* has finally arrived home. But her love and many warm memories remain.

I was so pleased that so many people recognised her quiet strength, her achievements, and her resourcefulness in their cards and letters, and at her funeral and celebration meeting.

You can read some of them at the end of the book.

Chapter 8

Pioneering With Women

Grace, the women's mentor

As our church in Chadwell Heath grew, Grace began preaching and quickly became an active speaker at women's meetings. And when we went to America, she heard and met some major women speakers.

She recalled, 'They inspired me to go for a wider ministry, not just to women but to mixed congregations. This was a breakthrough for me and the church. I wanted to model something for other women to follow, both those who were on leadership teams and those who weren't.

'I also started travelling to churches with Norman and began to meet other women who were potential leaders. I gradually started supporting them and caring for them.'

As a result, Grace quietly helped to pave the way for Christian women to lead and speak in what was then known as the 'house church movement'. And the ripples spread to almost every Christian denomination and stream.

She recalled, 'Before long, I held our first one-day conference in the south of England. More than 100 women spent the day together and had such a good time that the following year, 200 people came for a whole weekend.

'Then we started working in the north and saw hundreds of women gathering in Grimsby for the day. We had American speakers like Sandra Howells and Betty Jo Frank to encourage women into their ministries.

'Today there are many in leadership and ministry because of those times together. They were special.'

Job done

Grace felt she had completed her work with women when she organised a national women's meeting in Brentwood, Essex, in March 1990. Not bad for a woman without an education.

Coaches arrived from all over the country bringing more than 2,000 women for an inspiring, spiritual time.

Grace told me later, 'I could never have imagined all this would happen.' And a lot of other people found it hard to believe, too, as Grace wasn't the pushy, 'notice me' type.

She never demanded a platform or fought for 'women's rights' in the church. She just wanted to see women free to fulfil their hearts' desires. If that happened to be in leadership, then so be it.

As she once put it, 'Yes, of course, women should be able to lead, provided they get the job on merit.

But once they've got it, they shouldn't moan about the "time of the month".'

That attitude helped her to pioneer women's ministry in the UK.

Leading women worldwide

Grace was also part of a group of women that included people like Suzette Hattingh, who was part of Reinhard Bonnke's Christ for All Nations ministry team between 1980 and 1996.

This group pioneered women's ministry across the world. But Grace once confided in me, 'I was shocked to be invited. I never saw myself as important.'

Another time, she told a friend, 'When Norman and I first got married, I just expected to be a pastor's wife and help encourage women's ministry. I wouldn't have coped if God had told me what my future held. I never thought I would speak to crowds, visit war zones and jungles, and face all kinds of dangers.

'But it came naturally because if God sends you, he equips you. Fortunately, he created me to be adaptable. I can adapt to anything, anywhere. Which was just as well.'

She also served on boards with The Shaftesbury Society and Joyce Meyer Ministries UK.

What a testimony of how God empowered an 'ordinary', unqualified Cockney girl.

Grace preaching at a service at The Abbey Church, Azle, Texas

Chapter 9

Forming Links

The African connection

Early in 1979, we unexpectedly received a letter from a man in Ghana called Nicholas Andoh. We had never heard of him.

He had been given our names by a lady in Germany who had heard me speak. I'm not sure why, but she told him to contact me if he ever needed anything. He asked for our help. It sounded like he needed money.

I had been yearning to go to Africa for years, after having a dream about it. But I didn't feel any great desire to respond to this letter.

However, Grace and I prayed and chatted about it with friends, and eventually asked God to confirm the request by providing the air fare.

The money arrived from many different sources and was the largest gift we had ever received. Within six weeks we had £1,200, which was enough. So, I wrote and told Nicholas I was coming to Ghana.

The address he had given me was a PO box number, which turned out to be a sports stadium 180 miles from the capital, Accra. I didn't know if my letter would reach him.

But I booked the tickets, had the injections, obtained a visa and began the journey. It was as ordinary as it gets – a bloke from Dagenham nervously clambering up the steps of a plane, with his wife back home praying it would turn out OK.

However, I discovered on the plane that the Ghanaian government had closed the borders during a currency changeover. Planes and mail were not entering or leaving.

So, there I was, heading halfway around the world to meet a man I didn't know, and now I wasn't even going to land in the right place. I had to trust the Lord and see what happened.

Plenty happened, as you can see in our other book, *Destiny Calls*. It was an amazing trip that fulfilled many of our dreams.

When I got home, Grace and I went out and bought some items for a family I had met out there and we sent them off by freight. We didn't realise this simple act would develop into something much more significant.

A new normal

I would have been happy to call it a day after that first trip.

But you think differently once you have seen children without food, mothers without hope and fathers without work. That first journey couldn't be the last one. I had seen the needs, and I couldn't 'unsee' them. How could Grace and I go back to 'normal'?

Churches started giving us money, and eventually, we needed a separate agency to deal with it. Peter Martin, who was my close friend, administrator, and right-hand man, had a flash of inspiration. He suggested we start an organisation called Links International.

So, that's how Links was born, not with a fanfare, but with ordinary people like me, Grace and Peter meeting over a cup of tea and biscuits in a flat in Chadwell Heath.

That first trip grew into something beyond anything Grace and I could have imagined. Links now runs projects and supports people in 50 countries and turns over £1.3-1.5m a year.

And years later, Grace's funeral wasn't just a reunion of my blood family. It was also a reunion of the Links family.

People flew in from the USA and Ghana and travelled from Wales, Derbyshire, Yorkshire, Hampshire, Essex, Hertfordshire, Nottinghamshire and Birmingham (UK).

And Links will outlive both of us. That's the best bit.

Chapter 10

How Ordinary Are You?

One dream at a time

Grace and I found it hard to believe how God took a small operation like Links and used it in so many significant ways. And we also realised it was a doorway to greater experiences.

We ate bush rats and snails, were terrified by spiders, and used toilets that would make your hair stand on end.

We went up the Amazon, into the jungle, had an audience with the King of the Asante tribe in Ghana, met with the King and Queen of Romania, and stood on the Great Wall of China. And we were just this ordinary couple from Dagenham.

When Grace and I started out, we dreamed of inspiring people to give, to pray and to go. And when we grew older, we were still finding new situations, new challenges, and new opportunities, even though we didn't have official roles within Links. These continued, to the day Grace died.

Someone once asked us, 'How do you keep going?' We sometimes asked ourselves the same question. But let me tell you a story that helps to answer it.

A humbling example

Many years ago, I was asked to contact a lady called Shirley Chapman. She worked for Wycliffe Bible Translators in the Amazon jungle, and was home on furlough. I invited her for lunch and Grace put on one of her wonderful meals.

Shirley arrived at about 12.30pm and left at midnight. We had been asked to encourage her, but it turned out the other way around. Her story was both humbling and inspiring.

She had spent 30 years living and working among the Paumari tribe in the Amazon rainforest in Brazil. She and a colleague, a lady called Meinke Salzer, had given up their careers and their western comforts to live among this group of 800 people.

Shirley taught them the basics of health and hygiene, and how to read and write. She learned their language and became the first person to write it down on paper.

She also translated the New Testament into the Paumari language. It's called *God's Word on Paper*, and I have a copy of it in my flat. It was one of our most precious books.

I asked Shirley, who was in her 60s then, if we could support her. But she refused. Then I asked if we could visit her. And she agreed.

Shirley and Meinki lived in a house on stilts in the jungle, next to the Purus River, hundreds of miles from civilisation. They had no electricity, no running water and very few possessions. Their living conditions were basic. While we were there, we ate monkeys, turtles, and sea cow.

These two incredible women had also started a church among the Paumaris, and between 70 to 75 people attended. That's 10% of the population. Today, there are 800 in the church out of 1,200 in the tribe. That's a revival by any standard. We talk about church planting, but these ladies were doing it.

Shirley and Meinki deeply affected me and Grace. They were living examples of following a dream – ordinary folk, unsung heroes, affecting people's lives through their sacrifice. They were extending God's kingdom on the earth and making disciples in other nations.

They forfeited their own lives and careers and missed the chance to get married and have children. They had no platform, no recognition, and no glory. Just a life of serving others.

Grace and I later discussed what could happen if Shirley and Meinki were multiplied, hundreds of times over, across the world. Imagine the millions of lives that could be changed and the impact on communities and nations.

Grace was another unsung hero who was up to the challenge. And if she were sitting with you today, she would ask, 'What's your dream? Go for it. If I did it, so can you.'

No stranger to danger

Grace was quiet and petite but had remarkable courage and resilience. During five decades of ministry, she calmly faced dangers that would make most men and women tremble – or stay at home.

Once, she was trapped in a conference centre in Bangalore, India, for two days while mobs rioted and burned buses outside.

Another time, she travelled to Burundi during the bloody civil war between the Hutu and Tutsi tribes. She managed to get a ticket on a United Nations flight from Nairobi, and she left the day before the streets were mined.

And another time, she was trapped in a hotel in Sri Lanka while a gun battle raged outside.

And then, she was helped by an angel while travelling to Sri Lanka with two other women. They arrived to find civil unrest on the island. The atmosphere was tense among the crowds at the airport, and Grace and her friends resigned themselves to a long, hot and risky wait at customs and passport control.

Suddenly a man appeared out of nowhere, went up to Grace and her companions and told them to follow him so that he could show them a quick way out of the airport.

He led them around a corner, through a side door – and disappeared.

And the man who had been sent to meet them was standing there, ready to greet them. He had been waiting at the main entrance, but God had told him to meet his visitors around the side.

The only time Grace had felt afraid was when her boat was hit by a storm going across Lake Tanganyika in Africa. The craft lost its engine and corkscrewed in turbulent water for 15 hours in the pitch dark. Then it started leaking – a terrifying danger, with submerged rocks and hippos circling nearby.

Yet Grace hung in there, with immense courage and fervent prayer.

Fear not

That's how Grace faced life – and death. She said that she would die like Jacob who 'drew his feet up into the bed, breathed his last and was gathered to his people' (Genesis 49:33).

And that's what she did. She was calm, full of faith and thinking of others, right to the end.

Even after I left her bedside for the final time, she sent a nurse out with a message, reminding me to cancel her hair appointment.

Although she was in too much pain to preach in her latter years, she spoke to Freedom Church's women's group, Thunderbirds, on Zoom a few months before she died.

It was her final talk and she spoke about the blessings of having so many adopted children, and her determination to believe in God's promises, even when they weren't answered.

The women, all younger than her, were amazed by her zeal for God and passion for Jesus at the age of 86.

What a way to sign off from her preaching ministry.

Chapter 11

The American Dream

An ordinary couple in an extraordinary land

Over the years, Grace and I visited churches in American states including Texas, Oklahoma, New Mexico, Michigan, Indiana and Florida.

Grace dressed the part when we visited cowboy country in Texas 35 years ago

And because the work emerged from friendships, we were able to reach a whole range of denominations and groups – Baptists, Assemblies of God, faith churches and independent charismatic churches.

Grace and I in Texas 2005

ETERNITY CALLS

On a mission in Texas 2007

On a mission in Oklahoma

Many Americans found it hard to understand us to begin with – they had never met 'ministers' like us before.

This was because they were more used to 'The Prophet' or 'The Apostle' coming through, whereas we were just Norman and Grace from Dagenham UK, and we weren't sure whether we were prophets, apostles, or something else besides.

Christmas in Austin, Texas

Everything we did was based on relationships, and we ran a mile from being seen as 'big-name' preachers. And we paid our way to start with.

We preferred watching a movie while eating popcorn with a church's leaders than being 'super-spiritual' with them. But they took time to get used to this approach.

We were also happy to go to small churches as well as large ones, without looking to 'cover them' or 'own them'. We just wanted to be with them, and eventually, they wanted to be with us.

Golden celebrations

The warmth of these relationships was demonstrated when our American friends held a party to celebrate our golden wedding anniversary in 2014.

Our friends and family in the UK also wanted to celebrate with us, so we decided to hold parties in both locations.

The parties were very different and uniquely personal in their own way.

The 'local' one was held at Arun Church's Wickbourne Centre in Littlehampton. More than 200 people attended, and it was intimate, and riotous fun.

Grace spent her time catching up with old friends and family.

The American celebration took place in Azle, Texas, where we had ministered many times.

We were deeply moved that people flew in from all over America to be there. They represented almost every church we had worked with over three decades.

Sad farewells

We were aware that this would be our last time in America, and also the last time we would see many of these precious people until we got to heaven.

We felt it was important to say 'goodbye' properly, and we wanted to do it before it was too late.

Looking back, I am so glad we did. Grace revelled in the occasion, even though she couldn't understand why anyone would want to make a fuss of her.

The American people said goodbye to us in style.

They organised a gala dinner for about 200 people. The men wore evening dress, and the women wore gowns. Grace looked stunning in a cocktail dress.

Guests were greeted by valets who parked their cars. Then they entered the foyer to a string duo playing classical music and were greeted with hors d'oeuvres and wine.

The hall was decked with photos of us taken at different times in our ministry, and people were invited to take them home if they wished.

A professional singer sang Italian operatic arias, and, after the meal, there were prayers and speeches. Everyone wanted a photo taken with us. So, there we were, Norman and Grace from Dagenham, being treated like celebrities. It was like a dream.

And that was only half the story.

Mission accomplished

The following day, we were invited by Paul and Perrianne Brownback to minister at The Abbey Church in Azle, the first American church we had ever visited – and the last.

Grace and I receiving prayer from Perrianne Brownback and Jason Bollinger during our final visit to Texas in 2014

It was an emotional service. I preached on Acts 20:13-37, where Paul said goodbye to the Ephesian elders. There couldn't have been a more fitting subject.

And then came a big surprise. The pastor, Paul Brownback, presented us with an American flag that had been flown over the House of Representatives in Washington.

It had been arranged by Congresswoman Kay Granger and came with a framed certificate, thanking us for our service to her country.

Grace and I collapsed in a heap of tears. What an amazing tribute. It was only as time went by that we truly understood the flag's significance.

It's still on the wall of my flat, and I often look at it. It brings back such warm memories, not just of the party, but of decades of fruitful ministry in America with Grace…the Cockney girl who ended up being honoured by a congresswoman.

We were also presented with a globe made of mother of pearl, inscribed with the words, 'Your legacy to us means the world.'

More tears flowed.

So, we flew back to the UK with many emotions, and memories of working in dozens of churches in New Orleans, Dallas, Houston, Fort Worth, Lubbock and Amarillo (yes, we did know the way there!).

We had visited some of them only once, but formed deep and lasting relationships with others, seeing some through from 'birth' to 'adulthood'.

I think the American people realised that we weren't there to make money and that we weren't spiritual cowboys.

And we returned with a strong sense that we had completed our mission in America.

Roles reversed

However, the story continued. Since we 'left' America, at least 12 of our American friends visited us, including a team from Lubbock, Texas, who ministered at Arun Church while they were here.

We showed them some Sussex beauty spots and took them to other places. They loved it. And it was a great opportunity to pray with them and advise them.

Grace loved putting some of them up in our flat and providing wonderful meals, even though she found it harder in her latter days because she was in pain.

And the strength of those friendships was demonstrated when several people travelled from America to attend Grace's funeral.

They included Jason and Holly Bollinger, CEO of Links USA, Kerry Wood and Renaue Thompson. They wept with us at the crematorium and celebrated with us afterwards at the Littlehampton Academy.

And over the next few days, we spent some precious hours reminiscing about Grace in our flat.

I did my best to match her standards, but I suspect she was chuckling in heaven at my attempts to put together a buffet. However, I'm sure that she was delighted that some of her friends had travelled so far to say, 'See you later.'

Here we are with our dear American friends Jason and Holly Bollinger at Amberley Castle, West Sussex. They frequently came to visit us in the UK

Chapter 12

Later Years

Ministry at home

When we decided to 'retire', Grace and I weren't tempted to sit back and think, 'It's time to take it easy.' Thankfully, we were not like that.

We were both still dreaming of new things to do, new projects to accomplish, and new ways to serve the Lord, right up to the day she died.

It was only a year or so ago that we reflected on the fact that we had started off with a very broad ministry, like the base of a triangle. But, as we got older, our ministries became increasingly focused, until we became the apex of the triangle rather than the base.

This meant changes and cutting back on our workload.

Mealtime on our Mediterranean cruise

To begin with, we stopped travelling overseas. Then we laid down our national ministries and served mainly in our local church.

In 2005, God blessed us with a wonderful flat on the sea front, with a balcony overlooking the beach. We spent many happy hours gazing at the waves, families on the beach, surfers, and yachts with their brightly coloured sails.

On the ocean wave – together on a Mediterranean cruise in 2007

A new challenge

In 2007, David Thatcher, the pastor of Arun Church, asked us to look after the church's over-55s. We were overjoyed about having a new challenge.

We loved to be beside the seaside – in our flat in Littlehampton soon after we moved

We called the group Frontline, and it became established quite quickly. It initially attracted people over 65, as the younger ones didn't want to be associated with pensioners. But we soon had about 45-50 regular attenders.

The group soon became a comfortable place for people to engage in church life, and somewhere to bring their friends.

Grace and I outside a restaurant in Worthing, after an anniversary meal

Growing old gracefully

We also became active within the flats where we lived, and Grace loved caring for people and inviting them in. Our door was, as ever, always open and people frequently knocked to ask for help or a cuppa and a friendly chat – Grace's specialities!

And church people came for counsel, inspiration, and answers. We didn't always have those answers, but we tried to teach them how to be at peace with God when he was silent.

Someone once said to us, 'Thank you for modelling growing old.' We were a bit taken aback until they added, 'You have both maintained your enthusiasm, vision, passion and longing for the lost, the poor and the marginalised, and you are still breaking new ground.'

That meant a lot to us, especially on those days when we felt tired, and our joints ached.

Reaching out

During 2022, we had a dream of breaking bread with people who were unable to get to church meetings.

Grace was in a lot of pain from scoliosis by then, but we managed a few visits; she was determined to keep serving the Lord until the day she died.

We also started inviting young couples around for meals, and we learned so much from them and the issues they faced.

We also realised that when you reach your autumn years, you don't need a title like Pastor to minister effectively. Your ministry becomes one of influence.

We discovered that we could influence our own generation through our lifestyles, our attitudes and our willingness to discuss subjects like wills and dying that other people prefer not to mention.

Time to relax. Grace and I at Sheffield Park, East Sussex

Fostering young dreams

We also influenced young couples and teenagers by setting them an example and by inspiring them to chase their dreams. They saw us as spiritual parents, even though we didn't have our own children.

We told them that if we could live our dreams, so could they. After all, we never went to Bible college and were never ordained. And yet Grace became a nation changer.

She had a huge heart for young people and knew all their names. She watched them grow up, prayed for them, and eventually knew their babies' names, too. She longed to see them get hold of God's dreams for their lives.

Chapter 13

The End...and the Beginning

Celebrating Grace

On 14 October 2022, about 100 people gathered at Worthing Crematorium for Grace's funeral.

It was overwhelmingly sad, but also a time to celebrate the life of a wonderful woman who will now live for eternity.

Becca Jupp, leader of Arun Church, summed up her life with this tribute:

'Today we remember Grace, not just as a friend and mentor, but as a follower of Christ and a true leader. She led with truth, hospitality, faithfulness, joy, servanthood, humility, honour, love, deep loyalty and devotion.

'Grace wasn't just her name. It was who she was. It was her character...her very state of being.

'She was a free gift, given by God, and in turn, she gave freely to others for her whole life. Our unexpected loss is heaven's gain.'

And Jason Bollinger added, 'Our kids will miss the birthday cards that she unfailingly sent by Royal Mail. We will miss her bringing doilies from the States for the place settings at her table. We will miss her spectacular cackling laugh.

'We already miss her more than we ever imagined, but we are grateful for our time with her, her steady presence, leadership, and influence through the years.

'And while most of us have heard some of Norman's stories about the work of Links, there would be no Links without Grace's persistence and sacrifices.

'We will remember her in the words of 1 Timothy 1:14 in The Message, "The *Grace* of our Lord was poured out on me abundantly, along with the faith and love, that are in Christ Jesus."

'Even in these circumstances, we give thanks. We thank God for sharing her with us for 86 years. We honour and thank Norman for modelling with Grace a life and legacy of love, ministry, and missions that are a beautiful example for the rest of us to follow.

'Finally, we say, "Well done, Grace. Thank you for finishing your race like only you could. Your example as a faithful servant is something we will carry with us for all our days. Your legacy is more than you could ever imagine, and while we long to see you again, we love you, honour you, and thank you for everything you've done.

'We will now get on with God and practice everything you've taught us – including reading Psalm 91 together every day. We wouldn't be who we are without you!'

Grace was great

And then her sister-in-law, Christine Russell, paid tribute to her.

Christine said, 'Grace was a dear friend as well as my sister-in-law. I was introduced to her by her brother, Richard.

'Time passed by, and an opportunity was offered to them to help out at Chadwell Christian Mission. Things went so well there, that another opportunity presented itself for them to take over at the mission and move into the large flat above.

'Grace was in her element there. She could help people, invite friends and entertain them, something she took on board and perfected with great aplomb.

'My children, Grace's niece and nephew, loved to visit both Grace and Norman at the mission. There was a large garden in the grounds where they could run around and probably cause havoc. During school holidays when the children were a bit older, they couldn't wait to get there and stay for a week while I worked.

'Grace loved having them and spoiled them. They were allowed to pick fruit and vegetables from the garden. I'm not sure who enjoyed the experience most, the children or Grace and Norman.

'Grace would always say how her life would have been different if she had had children. But I'm sure she always knew she was destined for a different kind of caring life.

'A couple of weeks ago, Norman asked how many pairs of shoes I thought Grace had. My answer was 50, and he didn't confirm or deny this figure.

'Grace was addicted to shoes and had numerous pairs all neatly stacked in their original boxes in her wardrobe. I have known her to go shopping for a particular type of shoe to match a dress or bag. Then, while in the shop she would buy two pairs in different colours, just in case!

'I remember when Grace developed a bunion, and her favourite shoes, well, in fact, most of her shoes, became too painful and uncomfortable to wear. She couldn't wait for the surgery required to remove it. Surgery complete, she was back in those favourite shoes in a couple of months.

'Grace also loved clothes. Sometimes when I stayed with them in Rustington, West Sussex, we would walk to the village for some window shopping.

'Grace would say, "I'm just popping in this shop for a look." But she always came out with something, even if it was only a scarf.

'Sometimes we would walk arm in arm along the seafront, just talking. She would always be there as a shoulder to cry on or to help if I needed encouragement. She could also give me a good talking to if she thought it was necessary.

'Some of my best memories of Grace will always be her love of a good thunderstorm. She would stand on the balcony watching the ocean rolling in.

'If you had the pleasure of an invitation to a meal at the Barnes' household, be it breakfast, brunch, lunch, dinner or just a sandwich, it would always be accompanied by a linen napkin; no paper ones for Grace.

'I'm sure most of you would have heard the saying, "behind every great man there's a good woman".

'With apologies to Norman, Grace was a great woman.'

My tribute

In retrospect, it is not surprising that more than 400 people attended the celebration of Grace's life, organised by Arun Church shortly after her funeral.

And I read Jeremiah 1:6-9:

'Alas, Sovereign Lord,' I said, 'I do not know how to speak. I am too young.

'But the Lord said to me, "Do not say 'I am too young'. You must go to everyone I send you to and say whatever I command you. Do not be afraid of them, for I am with you and will rescue you."

'Then the Lord reached out his hand and touched my mouth and said to me, "I have put my words in your mouth."'

Then I said, 'Grace finished strong and served the Lord faithfully to the end. She found Christ when she was 12. Her ministry began when she was 33 and continued up until she died.

'She travelled all over the world, to 45 countries and she worked with Links in 84 different countries. Her influence was more far-reaching than she ever realised.'

Then I invited about 70 under-35s to stand and I prayed to commission them for their missions. It was a moving moment, and no one was more surprised than I was when they grouped around and prayed for me!

I sensed heaven's applause, and Grace was right there with that great cloud of witnesses, cheering us all on.

Grace understood the importance of finishing well. As one man put it, 'It's not how you start that matters, it's how you finish.'

Several people mentioned this at her funeral.

When I think back to those prayer meetings in the Elim Church in Dagenham, I realise that our dreams to reach out to the world were not illusions.

The Holy Spirit placed them there. The same as he has placed your dreams in your hearts.

Grace's legacy

Grace leaves an immense legacy.

I'm sure her hospitality, wisdom and directness will feature strongly, as well as the way she never let success change her.

She hoped that she would be remembered for leaving an understanding of the kingdom of God, a love of community, a heart for the poor, and a hunger for creativity.

And for seeing women discovering their ministries…and dreaming dreams.

Some of those dreams came to pass, sometimes in ways that we could never have imagined, and occasionally in ways we didn't particularly like. God surprised us, time and time again.

Other dreams are still being fulfilled in the lives of our many spiritual sons and daughters. And if you believe in generational blessings as Grace did, then many will be fulfilled, long after Grace went to glory.

In many ways, Grace was like the heroes of faith in Hebrews 11:13-16:

'All these people were still living by faith when they died. They did not receive the things promised; they only saw them and welcomed them from a distance, admitting that they were foreigners and strangers on earth.

'People who say such things show that they are looking for a country of their own. If they had been thinking of the country they had left, they would have had the opportunity to return.

'Instead, they were longing for a better country – a heavenly one.'

Even in the summer of 2022, Grace and I both felt excited about the future. We both knew that God was the God of new things, and we believed the best was yet to come.

For Grace, it really was.

Tributes to Grace

Renaue Thompson

Grace Barnes was a woman of practical yet indomitable faith. At a young age, she had determined that the enemy of her soul was never going to take ground in her life or the lives of those God gave her to love and shepherd.

Since she went to heaven the day after Queen Elizabeth II did, many have memorialised her as 'our queen' and, while I have no disagreement with that honour, for me, she was more of 'the Iron Lady'.

She had a will of forged steel and a warrior spirit that would not quit or relent until she saw God intervene in the lives of those she loved or evangelised.

Equally, she would not allow any pain or suffering of this life to interfere with her joy and purpose – she was determined in her heart to finish her course in God's strength and *that* she definitely accomplished!

Grace was a true friend and 'mother' to hundreds if not thousands of people in her lifetime. Her capacity to love was infinite, because she intimately knew the God of infinite, unfailing love.

Freely she received; freely she gave. If you were her friend or family, she loved you, corrected you, restored you, released you, championed you, hugged you.

Now it is up to us who remain to honour Grace Barnes as the Apostle Paul admonished us – follow the example she faithfully set, as she followed Christ's.

John Noble

More sad news!

I just received this message from Links concerning the passing of my dear friend Grace Barnes. I am so glad that I had the chance to have a meal with her and Norman recently.

Grace was faithful to the end, a fighter who never gave up, and a constant support for Norman through all the challenges they faced in their service to Jesus and the international communities they loved.

She will be sorely missed, but now we pray for Norman as he grieves and then moves on to discover the things the Holy Spirit will show him, as the Lord has not finished with him yet!

Their friend, John.

Dave Bilbrough

Very, very sad news. I've known Grace most of my adult life. Thoughts, prayers and love going out to Norman right now as he grieves.

John Games

A wonderful lady and faithful servant of our Lord. May Norman experience the peace and presence of the Lord in a special way.

Pauline Watts

Fond memories of Grace. She was an inspiration, a global citizen, and a blessing on the world stage. Praying for Norman as he navigates life without her and seeks God for the future. 🙏 ❤️

Sue Rinaldi

Very sad news. Many memories of Grace together with Norman visiting our church and conferences.

Mary Richardson

So sad to hear this. Grace Barnes was always a person with so much knowledge and so much love and compassion. She will be missed by all who knew her.

Though Grace might not have met Queen Elizabeth in life, she will in heaven, and I know the Lord will say 'well done, Grace, you fought the battle well' and now she is with our Lord crowned with ❤️ love.

Elizabeth Coveney

Another woman of faith, rooted in the earth, but connected to the heavens. A great example to us all.

Amanda Barker

Lovely memories of her and Norman. 💛

Chris Larkin

So sad. Memories of Grace going back 60 years. Amazing woman. We are blessed to have known her. ❤️

Raymond Lewis

Grace and Norman; two of the most beautiful people you could ever meet.

Andy Read

We honour her amazing life and legacy. Personally, I know I benefited from her faithful life of prayer. Grace – thank you, and I know I will echo the cry from heaven, 'Well done good and faithful servant. Enter your rest.' My love and prayers also, of course, to dear Norman.

Stuart Pascall

Sadness for those who remain to mourn; joy unconfined for the traveller who has finished the race!

Appreciative memories of the two of them from many years ago.

Maria Scard

I remember her kindness and lovely smile as well as her encouraging words. Thank you, Grace.

John Tancock

So sorry to hear this.

Terry Negus

Hi John, I was saddened to read of the death of Grace Barnes. I was friends with Norman from school days. We both lived in the same street but sadly we lost touch with each other. Please could you pass on my sympathy to Norman and assure him of my prayers at this difficult time. Terry Negus.

Shirley May Hardy

Beautiful lady. ❤️ I remember very special times with her. 🙏 Praying for Norman at this sad time xx.

Raymond and Chris Lewis

Grace and Norman – two of the most beautiful people you could ever meet. Their influence on our lives was so loving and encouraging over the past 30-plus years. Thank you, Grace, peace to you Norman. ❤️🤠👩🏻

Martin Higgins

A great lady who could speak directly into our lives will be missed. Our prayers to you, Norman.

Colette Lottie Nelson

So sorry to hear this today. She was an awesome woman and always brought something special when she and Norman came to Gateway x.

Anne and Pete Marshall

We remember her with affection. Praying for Norman that God will comfort him in his loss. With our love xx.

John Fletcher

Was saddened by the news today. At the Oaks Community church Dronfield, we have such wonderful and happy memories of Grace, her wisdom, love and sense of humour. Love to Norman at this time – in our thoughts and prayers.

Barbara Rogerson

Great memories.

Ruth Shepherd

She was precious; 🥹 glad I also got to hug her recently.

Pauline Duce

Lovely memories of a lovely lady.

Lorraine Maxelon

A privilege to have chatted to her recently. A great support to me in my early teens xx.

Cheryl-Charlie Collins

So sad to hear the news about Auntie Grace. Sending love and prays to Uncle Norman and family x.

Christine Catlin

Sad news. 2022 has been a year of losses xx.

Malc Garda

V sad news – much love x.

Gerry Smith

Sorry to hear this sad news x.

Sheila Garrod

Another beautiful gracious woman of God, gone to be with our Lord. My youngest has her name's sake in her with her middle name. Rest well lovely Grace x.

> **Robert Spinks**
> So sorry to hear of the sad news of our dear Grace, who demonstrated perseverance and love. Her cheerful laugh and disposition will always be in our mind, and her full dedication to you dear Norman throughout your ministry. Sending our love and prayers to you Norman. God bless you now immensely. Love Rob and Sue Spinks x

Chris Larkin

So sorry to hear that. Grace was an amazing woman. Praying for Norman xxx.

Claire Bell

We honour Grace; such a wonderful lady.

Andy King

Very sad news. An amazing woman of faith and we are so thankful for such a life well lived. Much love to Norman and all mourning her loss – you remain in our prayers. 💙

Sally Harman

Oh, so sad.

Bill Partington

So sorry to read this sad news – and so soon after her and Norman's anniversary. What a lovely lady.

We will be praying for Norman, and you all.

Alan Hoare

So sorry to hear this! Praying for Norman and the rest of you all.

Kathryn Ford

Sorry to read this. Praying and thinking of you all xxx.

Chris Leigh

Great memories of Grace at Riverside Church, Southwell.

Bekah Legg

Sending much love and remembering a real pioneer of women!! ❤️❤️

Yvonne Snyman

So incredibly sad. 💔

Jeannette Sax

A lovely tribute. Prayers and thoughts with Norman and all those who knew her x.

Paul Brownback

Heartbroken to hear this news. Such a life and legacy lived out in service to the Lord, the church and the poor around the world! She defined hospitality and its receptivity of others. She prayed like no other. We owe much of who we are to her leadership and prayer.

Colin Barnes

Thank God for Grace! ❤️

Fannie Pangani

Well done, Grace. Links will miss you and we appreciate you for all the sacrifices you made for Links to be where it is now.

Elizabeth Waim

Grace was amazing and an inspiration to us all, and, as Joe said, a prayer warrior! Praying for Norman and sending my love at this sad time x.

Kris Trammell White

Amen! ❤️ So blessed to have known and loved her!!! Our hearts are with you and Norman.

Jane Bennett-Neal

We will miss you so much, Grace. ❤️

Joan Thraves

Oh, bless her, now at peace. May our God of comfort be very present to Norman and all those who knew this most godly lady, Grace. 🙏❤️

Donna Kamentschuk

Oh, may God bless her and also be with Norman and his family at this very sad time.

Jo Williams

So sorry to hear of the sad news about Grace. My prayers for Norman and you all.

Jeff Summers

So sad to hear – sweet lady who blessed so many! Prayers for Norman!!! Hugs!!

Jeannie Benger

🙏💙

Jackie Elizabeth

💗

Flory Fuller

Loved and cherished, now missed forever ❤️. Rest in peace, lovely lady. God has earned another angel. 🥰🙏❤️

Aaron Colhoun

❤️✨❤️

Paul Marsh

May I take this opportunity to offer my condolences?

Donna Potter

Aww, so sorry to read this. She was a lovely lady, and she was like a grandma to me. I will miss the stories she always used to tell me and I will miss joining her for tea and biscuits. 🥲 🙏 Love u Norman and Grace x.

Yashwant Paul

Deepest condolences. RIP.

Janet Wright

A sad day, but she will remain in our hearts and her influence will continue on. She was one incredible lady.

Julie Bedford

❤️

Eileen Cooper

I remember Grace. She was an amazing person. God bless you Norman at this sad time. Love from Eileen. 🙏

Mark Wilson

God love, keep and bless Grace! Well done. Well done.

Norman, our hearts are with you, and we are upholding you in prayer. Call us anytime if there is anything we can do for you.

Love, Mark and Marion xxx.

Maria Del Pilar Barajas Gonzalez

Un gran ejemplo a seguir. Bendiciones. [A great example to follow. Blessings.]

Ruth Swaffield

So sorry to hear this news. Grace meant a lot to us. Thanks – for everything.

Jo Thorne

So sad. One of the most incredible women I have ever had the privilege to meet. She leaves part of her legacy in the lives of so many. Our condolences to you all and our love and prayers. 💜🙏💜🙏

Monica Garzon

Paz. psrs ella, pense que era noticia la reina isabel ya'esta como buemo con la reina.[Peace be with her, I thought that Queen Isabella was news, now she's with the Queen.]

Pete Gilbert

So sorry and so sad. Our thoughts and prayers are with Norman and you all.

Anna Elizabeth

Beautiful Grace, we love you and have been so very blessed to have known you. ❤️

Jennifer Copley

Praying for you all. 🙏

Kenneth Richardson

So very sad.

Claire Jones

So very sorry to read this news, but I know she is now in eternal glory with her saviour. Thank you, Grace, for your selfless love and faithfulness. You will be very missed. Love to you all and Norman at this sad time xx.

Richard At Oakscc Bull

A sad announcement for us, but a glorious day for Grace!

She ran the race well …

Sarah Belcher

So thankful for this wonderful lady, and sending love to you all x.

Judy Matthews

I'm personally so grateful to have known Grace; such an amazing lady who touched so many lives. Her legacy is great. Grace, you are now with our Lord and saviour. I shall miss you, until we get to meet again. Sending love and prayers for you all and especially Norman xx.

Beverley Hunt

Pleased to have met you xxx.

Love to Norman x.

Alison Wild

So sorry to hear this. Gracious Grace. What an amazing and special lady. So loved by Norman. Thinking of you Norman, much love.

Marji Weinmann-Buys

So sorry to hear about Grace. She was a beautiful lady. Her heart was gold. My heart breaks for Norman. Be strong. I know it's easy to say when your heart is breaking, but my prayers will be with you xxx.

Emmanuel Yambo

I remember her warm smile. That part of finishing her race got me!! Thank you, Jesus, for calling her home.

Ron-Annette Thiesen

Our deepest sympathy for all! 🙏🙏

Amy Wood

Beautiful soul who changed many lives, including mine. ❤️ Much love for you all as you mourn.

Jeff Lucas

So sad to hear this news. An amazing lady. Much love.

Yeison Valencia

Our condolences, 💐 brother, for the loss of this awesome woman. And thanks for all her investment in the kingdom of God. Love for all.

Links International – USA Office

Yesterday evening, 9 September, Destiny Called, and our Links family lost our matriarch, our spiritual mother, our prayer champion, and our biggest advocate. Grace Barnes finished her race and left this world to enter the eternal presence of Jesus.

Grace's life was a consistent and faithful testimony to the power and grace of God. From surviving the war as a young girl in London to following God's call to reach and minister to the nations, the impact of her life of service resonates around the world.

Grace lived with a courageous faith that has challenged all of us to greater things. Overcoming hardships and trials along the way, she never stopped pointing people to Jesus.

Our unexpected loss is heaven's gain. We are grateful for her steady presence, leadership and influence through the years, and there would be no Links without the persistence and many sacrifices of Grace. We join a grateful, global community in praying for Norman, her many friends, her spiritual brothers and sisters, sons and daughters, grandsons and granddaughters, and extended family.

Well done, Grace. Thank you for finishing your race like only you could. Your example of being a faithful servant is something we will carry with us for all our days. Your legacy is more than you could ever imagine, and we look forward to the day when we will see you again. We love you.

Zachary Nance

Oh my. How sudden. Praying for all those she touched. She has indeed finished her race and is now in the arms of Jesus.

Namara Laban

Sorry for the loss! RIP.

Kerry Wood

Grace was feisty, faithful and fearless. She didn't put up with much moaning or self-centredness, but she showed the grace of hospitality to all. What a trailblazer!! Praying for Norman and the church family that he and Grace so love.

Sandra Bullen

Sad to hear this news. Sending our love to you Norman xxx.

Hardy Jr Steen

God bless your family, Chip. I feel your loss.

Christine Lukadi

So sad to hear this news. RIP Mother.

Chris Russell

Grace meant so much to me. Both of you helped and prayed for me in the darkest days of my divorce, when I was broken. I was beyond grateful.

When you moved to Rustington, I wasn't sure we would be able to stay in touch, but Grace was key in making sure we did. I always loved to come and stay for a couple of days. Grace's hospitality knew no bounds. We would walk down to Look & Sea, arm in arm along the front.

Looking back to when I had to get a full-time job in London to support the children, both of you were there to take them in the school holidays.

I can tell you that both of them absolutely loved staying with you at the mission in Goodmayes. Again, I was grateful for your help.

As Grace had instructed 'no flowers', I thought a flowery card for you would be nice.

I first met you and Grace in late 1964, soon after your wedding. I think Grace and I got on straight away. When Richard and I lived in Bosworth Road, I recall the many times she would call in on her way home from her mum's. Mainly because she didn't have the bus fare to get home. It was a long walk. Richard always drove her home.

I am running out of space now, but I could say so much more. Lastly, my most favourite thing about

Grace was her linen napkins, be it breakfast, lunch or dinner – wonderful.

Dr Kerry Wood

I was a ripe old 27 years old when I first met Norman and Grace. I was discovering how lonely pastoral ministry could be, and the Lord responded to my prayer by sending Norman and Grace into my life.

At first, I thought her name was MyGrace. MyGrace, because Norman always referred to her as 'My Grace'. I thought, 'maybe that's a British thing.' I will admit I had trouble for years sorting out what was Norman and Grace and what was British. Still do.

They taught me so much about passion, mission, courage, and transparency. But, most especially, they taught me about relationship.

Lesson Number 1: relationships are expensive. They took my wife and I on a short vacation trip up through the Lake District, a boat on Lake Windermere, long winding narrow roads lined with stone, and pastures filled with sheep, (and, of course, hearing how old all these things were).

This was amazing to me – I had not even had that many vacations, much less with folks who weren't my immediate family. And I was so young, I probably didn't pay for a single meal. They were so gracious.

But I couldn't tell if they were constantly arguing, or if this was just the way the British do relationship! Grace was feisty! She would listen to Norman, and then listen some more…then she would give her perspective! And when she did, she would finish most sentences with the question, 'Didn't we Norman?' It was sweet and gracious beyond words.

I wasn't sure if this was feminism, just British, just Grace, or pure holiness. But I was learning what relationship is, and that it is expensive.

We finished up that day's drive in Carlisle. As soon as we checked into the hotel, Grace was given a message that her mum had fallen and broken her hip. Grace immediately returned home to care for her mum. Grace had a grace for carrying burdens. Hers was not an easy life – but a courageous life.

Revelation 1, John talks about the 'tribulation, the kingdom, and the patience of the Lord Jesus.' As I've reflected on Grace's impact upon my life, these words best describe her to me.

She learned through the years, after a difficult childhood, how to receive the grace of the Lord Jesus in tribulation. She grew bold and powerful in the authority and life of the kingdom (which included amazing hospitality). And, I think, most remarkable in her life was the demonstration of the incomprehensible patience of Jesus.

I remember at the end of one particularly challenging leadership meeting in Texas, which went on and on, she said, 'Well, at the end of the day" (a very British saying to us in the States). 'Well, at the end of the day, it's the end of the day.'

And then she laughed in that joyous, free expression of hers. Grace has been a light for all of us in the tribulation, the kingdom, and the patience of the Lord Jesus. God's continued grace upon you and with you, my dear friend, Norman.

Keith and Sarah Unwin

Grace had such a lovely way of making people feel valued and loved. We feel privileged to have known her and send you our love, thoughts and prayers at this difficult time. It seems that there are now two Queens in heaven this week!

Linda Harding

I have many memorable moments of the impact of Grace in my life. Her love, her authenticity, her conviction, her open heart, her humility, her courage, the joy she carried. Above all, she was "GRACE" – by name and nature. Always an inspiration 😊. What a legacy she leaves – and I pray the impact of her 'life lived to the full' will last for many generations.

Andrew and Mavis Rackstraw

Our abiding memories of her were to do with her gift of hospitality. 'Come 'n go where you like, poke around a bit' was her greeting when we visited your home in Goodmayes many years ago. She was a great homemaker and always keen to share it with anyone who turned up. Grace made everyone welcome.

Stephen, Megan and Anna Taylor

She brought life into our lives, and we are gutted! That Grace is free from pain and in the best place ever now, we are thankful to Jesus!

Jenny and Adrian Oliver

Grace was such a wonderful lady, so faithful, cheerful, caring and giving. Together you formed a truly amazing and inspiring couple whom God clearly brought together to fulfil a destiny.

Molly Bell

What an inspirational lady your Grace was! She touched so many lives around the world by just being the amazing woman of God that she was, a real life-changer, particularly for women, wherever she went.

Graham and Val Howell

We were very privileged to have known Grace, and to have you both stay with us and also becoming very dear to us.

Knowing how immaculately Grace kept her home and excelled in hospitality, she also was a perfect guest, and we loved having her with us.

I went to three of Grace's ladies' days, one in the village hall at Ravenshead. We were touched and changed. She had a real heart to see lives set free and achieving their full potential in God.

Grace gave of herself, putting others before herself. An amazing example of humility and a life of service for her Lord.

David Thatcher

Such lovely memories of Grace, unique and beautiful in every way. A mother to so many, encouraging me even last Sunday in her own, inimitable way.

I am so thankful to God for Grace's steadfast and exuberant faith in God, in Christ.

I am so thankful that you both came among us and together loved and supported this church and its leaders from the very first. What an amazing couple, and what an inspiration Grace has been.

She had lived a long life in loyal obedience to God, with an influence that is far-reaching.

Paul and Su Read

We always knew from the Bible that sometimes God woke his servants up in the middle of the night to tell them something, but we learned from Grace that that was something God did in the 1980s too.

Grace was a listener and a pray-er and it was because of her listening and praying that we have this story to tell.

If you've read the book *Destiny Calls* you will know part of our story…we are the Paul and Su who had a premature baby whose cord was wrapped four times around her neck at birth.

'Inexplicably,' the baby's arrival was four weeks early and the midwives, realising what was going on at the sharp end, told me, 'Su…stop pushing…we have something to sort out here.' They sorted it out…untangled our baby before she was completely delivered, and we had the happy ending.

Norman and Grace were among the first people we told of our daughter's sudden arrival; in fact, we phoned to tell them we were going into hospital at around 2am to ask them to pray (you did that sort of thing to your church leaders in those days!). We were so scared.

Afterwards, when they visited me in the maternity ward, they shared that God had woken Grace up in the night early in our pregnancy with a warning that our baby might die.

As a result, they prayed for us and for our unborn child every single day, so it wasn't 'inexplicable' that I went into early labour; it was a testimony of Grace's listening and God's faithful kindness and mercy. The fact is that, if the pregnancy had gone full term, our daughter would very likely have been strangled at birth…or even before.

We named her Natalie Grace…but here comes the bit that's not in *Destiny Calls*. People might think we gave her Grace's name *after* the baby was born, in gratitude when all was safe and sound. But not so. Paul and I decided early in the pregnancy that – if the baby was a girl – we would like to name her for Grace.

We thought we had better go and ask her if that was OK…so I did. You know what Grace was like …I was expecting her to get all emotional and at least say, 'Oh Su, love…' and give me a hug (you can imagine) but nothing quite like that. She was pleased, but her response was uncharacteristically muted, to say the least.

Afterwards, Paul said, 'How did it go?' and I said, 'Well…I think she was happy…she seemed a bit quiet about it.' Of course, what we didn't know was that we had asked her *after* God had woken her up in the night, and I think that makes Grace all the more special. She didn't betray even so much as the tiniest hint of what she believed God had said…and she kept that counsel for the full eight months of our pregnancy...trusting God's goodness, while probably surreptitiously watching me like a hawk.

We are part of each other's faith journey. For Grace, this was a test that she passed with flying colours. She proved that she was someone God could trust with a secret, and we will be – literally – eternally grateful.

Maurice and Wendy Adams

You have both been highly significant in so many lives. Most probably, more than you even know about. Personally, we are honoured to have known Grace as 'Grace' – but also the remarkable couple of Grace and Norman.

Wendy still remembers the trip to Burundi with Grace, and how at ease Wendy felt sharing time and ministry with her. Grace's kindness, support and wisdom shone brightly.

And the special memories when you both came to visit us in Zimbabwe and Uganda.

What faith. What faithfulness.

John and Christine Larkin

Grace was a role model and an encouragement to me at the time, but the most touching memory was when I joined her on a three-week trip to India, and we shared a room up in the hills, with no toilets or running water, and she was amazing. She made me laugh every single day with her observations, comments and stories.

As many will have said in tributes, emails or messages to you, Grace lived life to the full, and well. The seeds sown from her life will go down generations.

Margaret Togwell

I still occasionally think of Grace's instructions when I am ironing a shirt, and how I had to starch your collars and cuffs. I was extremely nervous when I ironed your shirts that I wouldn't do it properly!

Also, memories of the cleaning, and how Grace wanted one of her rooms spring-cleaned every week in rotation, and we helped her. Us girls always said that your house was much cleaner than any of ours! (Not that ours were dirty). We were taught well!

Chris and Nicky Pearson, Joshua and Grace

We will always remember Grace as a beautiful lady, who blessed our family by praying for our children for over 30 years. They were both serving God full-time. Thank you as a couple for all you've done for the world.

Sue and John Smith

Dear Norman,

Words cannot express our sadness when we heard of Grace's unexpected death. We only saw you both sitting on your balcony together a couple of weeks ago when we passed by.

Grace truly was a remarkable woman, and we were honoured to have known her. We connected on our first meeting as 'old Londoners' and had a few chuckles together.

We send our love to you, and we pray that you will find the Comforter in a tangible way as you walk through these difficult days of mourning the loss of your soulmate.

With our love.

Linda and Richard, Ella and Jacob and Alfred Bless

Dearest Norman,

We are so sad to hear this news of dear Grace being called home to be with Jesus. What a shock.

Seeing Grace recently at Christine's celebration of life reminded me of how beautiful and graceful Grace was.

She was an amazing woman's role model. A true legend.

You must be devastated, and we can't imagine the pain of your separation.

We are sending our huge love and prayers to you at this difficult time.

With huge love xx. (I'll fish out some lovely photos of Grace with Ella when she was a toddler).

Richard and Karen Bull

Hi Norman,

We have just heard the sad news of Grace's passing.

We are so sorry for your loss.

She was one of our heroes, along with yourself, and she will be sorely missed by thousands, and mostly missed by one; yourself.

Although it's a sad time, it's not a bad time – she has passed on to be in heaven's peace and glory, to be continually in the very presence of Jesus. Grace, we salute you.

And Norman, we are praying for your comfort in grief, and joy despite the sadness.

We love you both.

Dave and Pat Bilbrough

So very, very sad to hear this news just now, Norman. Grace lived such a great life caring for others. Furthering the gospel in so many parts of the world and, of course, devotedly supporting you in your many initiatives together.

It must be such a shock and such a huge loss to you as we know how compatible and formidable the two of you were together.

Right now, sending huge amounts of love, empathy and solidarity to you as you grieve.

Bob and Penel D

Such good memories of Grace. A woman of wise counsel and full of the Holy Spirit.

We loved those brief times shared with you both and the turning points you initiated in our lives. Grace was to you as Prince Philip was to the Queen, a great backer up and encourager.

Our love and prayers are with you at this time.

Martin and Gayle Scott

Huge condolences in your personal loss. A race run to the end, till death.

And now, having passed on, Grace will still speak through the seeds sown in hearts, lands, and connections, and she will speak because they were seeds for the future, drawn from the sacrifice of the cross.

Blessings on you in abundance.

Pastor Phil Taylor

May God's grace, presence and peace comfort and surround Norman and the entire family! Grace was such a precious lady. We sorrow in our loss but rejoice in heaven's gain.

Chris and Susannah Catlin

River Church Bristol.

It is with sadness that Susannah and I have learned of the passing of your dear Grace.

We recall many years ago how you both helped us with clear wisdom and encouragement in the mission, sending over your wonderful parcels to us missionaries in Mozambique.

On returning to the UK, we were hosted by you both, and Grace cooked us wonderful meals. What a true servant of the Lord.

We pray that you will be strong, Norman, and trust God's leading and his bountiful grace will continue with you.

Jane Mettam

Have just received the news from Links that Grace has gone to glory. What a lovely tribute to her in the email.

What can I add but to say thank you to God for her strong faith and welcoming heart. Her love and care was always so evident every time we chatted when you both came up to Dronfield. It was a privilege and godly education to have gone to Mexico with her all those years ago.

May Jesus' peace and comfort rest on you and those she knew so well.

Terry and Denise

Hello Norman, so sorry to hear about Grace, such a lovely lady. You are in our thoughts and prayers. She loved Jesus and it is good to know she will be with him now in heaven.

All our love Norman, as always.

Barry and Rowena McKnight

We were sad to hear of your bereavement.

What a wonderful tribute to Grace by Links International. She was greatly used by God throughout her life, and she will be greatly missed. But we can praise the Lord that she will now be enjoying her reward in heaven, at last in the presence of Jesus.

We feel for you, Norman, at this time of loss, and we will be praying for you.

Trevor Perkins

I am very saddened to hear of Grace's passing. She was a kind and gracious lady and I thank the Lord that I have had the enormous privilege of knowing her, and Norman, personally. The good news is that she is with the Lord.

My prayers go to Norman during his grief at the loss of his devoted partner, and to all of you at Links who knew them well and will miss them very much.

Dawn and Ivan Kerridge, Paul and Angela Ashton, and Anne Woods

Sincere and heartfelt condolences from us all on your loss. Our family has the fondest memories of Grace, a truly lovely lady. We know she will be very much missed.

🫶❤️

Peter and Kay Goodchild

Dear Norman,

We send our love to you dear brother at this tough time, and we thank the Lord that we ever met you both. It's been a while since we were last with you, but we think of you often. At Mike's funeral I believe (?). You were so blessed with Grace, and we have always thought of you as a great and unique team together.

Sending love to you, Norman, from our home in South Africa while we are serving in Emmanuel Press.

We pray for Father's deep peace over the coming days and weeks, and we look forward to seeing you again.

Jesus bless you, dear brother!

Jan, Richard, Lydia, Andrew, Paul, Anna and Tim Williams-Menlove

We have so many memories going back over the years; Dad introducing you and Grace to the mission is where it all began.

Our lives took different paths, but both of you were just a call away. Thank you both for your love and prayers. We will miss Grace, but the memories remain. We send you all our love and prayers.

Sadly, we will not be able to join in the celebration during the evening as it is a long way to travel from Derbyshire, and Richard is not too well.

We were thrilled to have Norman and Grace with us for a meal just before Christmas when they were staying with friends in Sheffield. Our friendship goes way back with my dad introducing Norman to the 'mission'.

Although only a few years younger than Norman, I was one of the young people! The early mission days were a great time, and we have many happy memories. Richard was involved with John Noble and, when we married, we joined with the 'house church' as it was first known.

I have known John and Christine since I was about 12. Christine met my mum in the local store and Mum invited them for tea, and Dad was privileged to lead John to the Lord. So, a little bit of history!

Russ Holmes

Greetings Norman,

I am so sorry to hear of the passing of your lovely wife. Grace was a true inspiration, and she touched the lives of so many through her ministry with you.

Praying blessings over you as you grieve and that he would be close to you and bring comfort.

Many blessings.

Phil and Diane Streeter

Our dear Norman,

The news was so sudden. Two Queen of Hearts suddenly relinquishing their lives in two days! Having gazed upon Grace's face and listened to her laughter just a few days before, and now the shock of her rapid departure!

Along that crowded road of cherished memories, she has planted many signposts on the way. Her wide smile, easy relaxed conversation, the sparkling sincerity of her faith in God, her Great Enchanter, and her acute insight into people's problems and wisdom in untangling them.

With the Grace we fondly remember, there was never a drop of self-pity but a constant giving of herself to the joys and griefs of others. Diane remarked on her own sense of inner joy when conversing with Grace during the coffee afternoon that we so recently shared with one another. Now

Grace has gone, but not without leaving a flicker of light on a rose-covered wall.

A massive part of your life has ended, Norman, and we grieve for you in your pain, heartbreak and loss. At the same time, *not* praying that God will give you comfort and consolation in your loss; if he did that, Grace would no longer live vividly on in your memories.

Masses of affection during this period of inexplicable anguish.

FESODEV staff, Malawi

We at FESODEV in Malawi would like to send condolences to Norman for the loss of Grace. We are saddened by the loss of our mother, our visionary.

May her soul rest in eternal peace.

Charles and Paula Slagle

Grace was an amazing lady, and I know the Lord has joyfully welcomed her with open arms and that she is rejoicing in his presence, even now.

But she will be greatly missed by those of us left here, who had the honour and blessing of knowing her.

In his love.

Phil Togwell

Grace and Norman played such an important role in my early years. Following her divorce, my mum searched for somewhere to feel safe, to recover, to heal…and she found Chadwell Christian Mission, which Grace and Norman were leading at the time.

I must have been around eight years old, and the church probably only numbered 20 or 30 people. But they cared for my mum, my sister and I. They offered the hospitality that we all so desperately needed. I know that Grace and Norman regularly prayed for me, and I have no doubt that their prayers have shaped some of who I am today.

I am deeply grateful for Grace's life and witness, and I am praying that Norman knows the peace and comfort of the Holy Spirit as he mourns.

Paul Titus and team, Joy Counselling Consortium, Kenya

Here in Kenya, we received the news of Grace's passing on with sadness. We are, however, greatly encouraged to know she has gone to be with the Lord Jesus our saviour.

Links International, which Norman and Grace started, has helped to change many lives here. We have seen a great transformation in our community. Their vision and sacrifices continue to inspire us.

We stand in prayer with Norman and the entire Links family. May our Lord give you all strength, peace and comfort during this difficult time.

Please, find comfort in Revelation 21:4, 'God will wipe away every tear from their eyes; and death shall be no more, neither shall there be anguish, sorrow and mourning, nor grief, nor pain any more, for the old conditions and the former order of things have passed away'.

Christine Gibbard

Dear Norman, I am sending my heartfelt sympathy and prayers for you on the tragic, unexpected passing of your dearest wife and partner in the Lord.

What a life and witness! I know you will be heartbroken but strong in the comfort and total faith in knowing that she is in glory and without pain.

Sending love and thanks for the sacrifice you made in meeting us that day.

Geoff and Pauline Williams

We were so sad to hear of the 'home call', of your dear Grace. However, she is in the best place, in the presence of the King.

Although that is greatly comforting, there is the area of human sorrow, and we know how you will be missing your dear Grace, a wonderful lady and servant of the Lord. Many will be thankful that she crossed their paths. Her memory will live on in the hearts of countless numbers.

May you know the comfort and strength of the Lord, as you, along with valued fellow workers, continue with the ministry of Links. We do get the information, so seek to keep in touch.

With increasing age, may the Lord give you his strength to continue. As we are in our late eighties, we have had to review what we can and can't do, so travels overseas have had to cease.

We are thankful for the computer and email, so seek to keep in touch with folk, worldwide. My (Geoff's) great-grand-aunt married Charles Babbage, the 'father of the computer', a wonderful invention. How thankful we are for it.

Blessings in Christ and our love.

Edward, Edfri International

To all our friends of Links International Family,

We join you in celebrating a life well lived of our sister in Christ and co-worker in the work of the gospel, Grace Barnes. Your great tribute caught my attention in two ways, that:

1. Actually, we are called to find our purpose in God and by the grace given and being able to live to the fullest and accomplishing that purpose, until destiny calls us home.

2. It's about the legacy we follow. Paul in 2 Timothy 4:7, 'I have fought the good fight, I have finished the race, and I have remained faithful' is about legacy, as we join you in celebrating a life well lived.

We also use this opportunity to let our friends in the UK know that you all remain in our thoughts and prayers as you mourn the passing away of Her Majesty Queen Elizabeth II. What an amazing icon she was, a true symbol of a godly monarch.

God be with you as you reflect on the lives of the two great women of God.

Very much in our thoughts and in our prayers.

Robin and Margaret Aim

Dear Norman and Links International friends,

Our condolences to you all, especially Norman, on the loss of Grace – we remember her as a lady whose name fit her well. I know you will all miss her so much.

Jochen Tewes, Secretary, Inter-Mission Industrial Development Association

It is with sadness that we received the note here in India about Grace Barnes' call to her eternal mansions; Grace who was a co-founder of Links International.

Although we know that these mansions are our destiny, too, we will still miss her, particularly those of us who received so much encouragement from her through her life, love and service.

We are praying for you all and particularly for Norman, to whom I sent a personal message.

Loving greetings in the Lord.

Cherie and Mick Down

We were so very sorry to hear the sad news about Grace.

She has been an inspiration and example to us and to everyone at the Oaks for over 40 years, and it has been a privilege to know her.

Mick and I have felt especially blessed to have met with you and Grace each year at The Big Church Day Out, until Covid put a two-year pause on it and prevented us going this year too.

We are so sorry for your loss, and we send you our deepest sympathy.

Jayne Lindsell

Dear Norman,

I wanted to send a message to you at this sad time. But it's not sad for Grace, as she has been called home to where her Lord had a place prepared for her – and for us too. Hooray.

Although I have not seen you both since the handover at Harlow from Peter and Suzanne to Brian and Mary, a while back, I think of you often.

Travelling with you to Ghana all those years ago and getting to know you there has been a real shaping experience in my Christian life. You both taught me so much about how to relate to brothers and sisters of another culture.

And then, going on to learn how to lead women's meetings from Grace when I could hardly dare to speak into a microphone was so very helpful.

Both of you demonstrated to me how you can lead by being kind and humble. I will never forget Grace in Ghana asking us ladies if we had any knickers to wash as she was doing hers!

So, I send you my love and prayers xxxxxx.

Ebby and Hope Jupp

Dear Norman,

Hope and I would like to extend to you our deepest and most sincere sympathy on the home call of dear Grace, your beloved companion for so many years.

We were just beginning to come to terms with the death of our Queen when the news came through of your dear one's passing, which brought home to us the confirmation of the glorious hope we have as believers in the saving power of our God.

We are sure you will be conscious of his comfort and sustaining grace in these days and know that our beloved church family, of which you are such a valued member, remains behind you and will continue to pray for you.

We thank God for Grace's life and constant and faithful witness to the love of her saviour. We will so miss her.

Michael Scutt

Hi my old friend,

Do you remember when you, Grace, Jennifer and myself met on the isle of Wight on 5 September; both on our wedding days! Way back in 1964 (or was it 1965?)

Take care my long-remembered friend. I remember Grace said one day on that holiday, 'If Norman stood upright on the beach with a towel held to his chest, he could be a flag post'!

Also finally, you had been there for barely a couple of hours, when we heard laughter coming from the hallway outside our room. Apparently, the heavy toilet seat had fallen down as you flushed it, and a big chunk of the toilet bowl was tipping out.

Again, thinking of you preaching at my dad's church in Acton – lots of memories and stories.

Sue France Junior (John's wife)

Dearest Norman,

It is with deepest sadness that I write to you.

Although, with thanks and rejoicing, Grace is now with her Lord and saviour.

However, I feel so much for you losing your life-long love and soulmate.

You have been such a godly example to us all for many decades.

And I will never forget all the foundations you laid in John's and my life in the 1970s as newly-weds, along with Grace's sense of humour, honesty and that spark in her eyes.

Grace taught us much about living out the nitty gritty of our Christian walk in a godly way, having regular date nights and looking good when our husbands came in from work, along with many, many other really important things that became part of our life routine, and which we have been able to pass on to our children and grandchildren.

She was a real trophy of the grace of God in action.

We always loved to see you when you called in to see us in Rotherham.

And I am so glad that we were able to see Grace when you were recently up at Wendy's in Sheffield.

The days ahead will inevitably hold tough moments as you face life without her. But I pray that you will find God to be your comfort in ever-increasing ways and that he will be your compass at this time, as he has been your whole life through.

Well, Norman. Sending love and prayers. Thinking of you.

Teresa Knott

Dear Norman,

It was an honour to know Grace, and yourself.

You inspired us so much, and we were so blessed by your prophecy over us, and the ministry God laid in our hearts.

I send you my love and prayers as you journey through your loss. Yes, I know Grace is home with our Lord and has life eternal and that one day we will be reunited, but I also know how hard it is initially to come to terms with not having your beloved partner beside you.

Our hope is in the Lord, and comfort and strength pour out through family, friends and church, but, ultimately, it is the Holy Spirit that dwells in us that gently holds us as we grieve.

It is so special to have a marriage that is Christ-centred and to grow in the Lord together through the blessings and trials of life. You were a chord of three strands and, as Grace humbly walked beside you with her faith and trust in Jesus (no matter what this life challenged you with), lives across the world have been transformed through the grace of God.

My constant prayers are with you, Norman, as you have the funeral and memorial celebration service for a beautiful woman of Christ, your beloved Grace.

God bless.

YOUTH

Naomi

I want to start off with saying I am so sorry for the loss of Grace. From what I know, she was an incredible woman, and she will be so dearly missed.

You probably don't remember, but I was one of the students in the word at TLA, when you came and told us all your story and showed all the pictures. I remember being absolutely blown away by the incredible life that you and Grace had been through, and all the things that you accomplished together. You and Grace impacted so many people's lives, and you should always remember that.

I can't even imagine how hard it must have been for you to lose her, but we need to remember that she is in a better place now, free from pain and suffering. I hope you know that we are all here with you, praying and supporting you through this.

All of my love, thoughts and prayers.

Red

My favourite part of the word was when you and Grace would come in to tell us stories of your travels and spreading the word of God.

Thank you for everything you have done for the community and more.

Elijah and all of us

In this rough time, please remember that God is with you in the good and the bad and everything in between and all of us will always be with you.

Zion and Luca

Dear Uncle Norman,

Thank you for always asking me how football went; even if I lost, you would encourage me.

Elyana

To Uncle Norman,

I just want to tell you that I'm so thankful for everything you and Auntie Grace did for us. You both were such an amazing couple. I have loved all your amazing stories. You have both built my faith so much.

Thank you for all those delicious waffles and for inviting us over around Christmas and for always remembering our birthdays. I loved Auntie Grace so much.

Chloe

Dear Norman,

I am so sorry for your loss.

I didn't know Grace personally, but she seemed like a joy to have around.

We will all miss her a lot.

Printed in Great Britain
by Amazon